THE BOOK OF...

WHERE?

KINGFISHER
NEW YORK

KINGFISHER
LONDON & NEW YORK

Copyright © Kingfisher 2011
Published in the United States by
Kingfisher, 175 Fifth Ave.,
New York, NY 10010
Kingfisher is an imprint of
Macmillan Children's Books, London.
All rights reserved.

Distributed in the U.S. by Macmillan,
175 Fifth Ave., New York, NY 10010

Illustrated by Ray Bryant
Concept by Jo Connor

Library of Congress Cataloging-in-Publication
data has been applied for.

ISBN 978-0-7534-6598-1

Kingfisher books are available for special promotions and
premiums. For details contact: Special Markets Department,
Macmillan, 175 Fifth Ave., New York, NY 10010.

Printed in China
10 9 8 7 6 5 4 3 2 1
TTR/0511/LFG/UNTD/140MA

WHAT'S IN THIS BOOK?

WHERE...

6   ... DID THE DINOSAURS GO?

7   ... CAN YOU SEE RIVERS OF ROCK?

8   ... DO BABY SHARKS LIVE?

9   ... DO ANGELS, CLOWNS, AND PARROTS LIVE?

10   ... DO I GET MY BALANCE FROM?

11   ... DO ELEPHANTS GLOW IN THE DARK?

12   ... DO BEARS GO IN THE WINTER?

13   ... IS THE WORLD OF THE ICE GIANTS?

14   ... IS IT NIGHT ALL DAY LONG?

15   ... IS THE TWILIGHT ZONE?

16   ... MIGHT YOU FIND A PHARAOH?

17   ... ARE THE PYRAMIDS?

18   ... DO RAINBOWS HAPPEN?

19 . . . DOES IT RAIN FOR A MONTH?

20 . . . DOES CHOCOLATE GROW ON TREES?

21 . . . DO PLANTS GROW?

22 . . . DOES MY FOOD GO?

23 . . . DO INVENTORS GET THEIR IDEAS?

24 . . . DOES COAL COME FROM?

25 . . . CAN I SAVE ENERGY?

26 . . . DOES UNDERWATER GRASS GROW?

27 . . . IS THE BIGGEST CORAL REEF?

28 . . . IS THE BIGGEST ANIMAL?

29 . . . DOES THE BIGGEST REPTILE LIVE?

30 . . . IS THE LONGEST RIVER?

31 . . . DO ANGELS FALL?

32 . . . DOES THE SUN GO AT NIGHT?

33 . . . DO KOALAS LIVE?

34 . . . IS THERE LAND BUT NO COUNTRIES?

35 . . . WAS THE HEAVIEST SNOWFALL?

36 . . . DID BIRDS COME FROM?

37 . . . ARE DINOSAUR FOSSILS FOUND?

38 . . . ARE THE HIGHEST MOUNTAINS?

39 . . . DOES THE WIND GET THE WINDIEST?

40 . . . DOES IT NEVER RAIN?

41 . . . ON EARTH SIZZLES THE MOST?

42 . . . WOULD YOU FIND A RUNNING PLANT?

43 . . . WERE THE FIRST OLYMPICS?

44 . . . IS THE EYE OF A HURRICANE?

45 . . . DO EARTHQUAKES HAPPEN?

46 . . . WOULD YOU FIND A FLYING WEAVER?

47 . . . DO BIRDS LIVE IN CITIES?

48 . . . ARE RAINFORESTS?

49 . . . IS THE BIGGEST FOREST?

50 . . . IS THE LONGEST CAVE SYSTEM?

51 . . . CAN YOU PLAY SPORTS IN A CAVE?

52 . . . DO WOMEN WEAR DERBY HATS?

53 . . . DO MEN WEAR SKIRTS?

54 . . . DID CHINA COME FROM?

55 . . . DOES IT TAKE HOURS TO DRINK TEA?

56 QUICK-QUIZ QUESTIONS

58 QUICK-QUIZ ANSWERS

60 TRICKY WORDS

62 WHERE TO FIND STUFF

64 FAREWELL

HAVE YOU EVER ASKED YOURSELF WHERE?

It's only natural to be confused by the world around us . . . It is a very complicated and surprising place sometimes! And you'll never understand what's going on around you unless you ask yourself "WHERE?" every now and then.

"Where" is what this book is all about.

We have traveled over the land, under the sea, up mountains, across deserts—and even into spooky caves—to collect as many tricky questions as we could find . . .

. . . and we also found the answers for you!

We now invite you to come with us on our journey around the world of "WHERE" so that we can show you all the answers we discovered.

We also thought it might be fun to see how much of this shiny new knowledge you can remember—go at the back of the book, on pages 56 and 57, you'll find some Quick-Quiz questions to test you out. It's not as scary as it sounds—we promise it'll be fun. (And besides, we've given you all the answers on pages 58 and 59.)

While we were searching for all those answers, we found out some other pretty interesting things, too. We wrote them all down on these panels—so you can memorize these facts and impress your friends!

Did you know . . .

The biggest bat colony is in Bracken Cave, Texas. More than 20 million bats roost there.

Are you ready for this big adventure? Then let's go!

WHERE DID THE DINOSAURS GO?

Around 65 million years ago, the dinosaurs vanished. Scientists think that Earth was hit by big rocks from outer space, causing dust clouds to block out the Sun. Plants died, then plant-eating dinosaurs, and then meat eaters.

Did you know . . .

It was not only the dinosaurs that died out 65 million years ago. All of the flying reptiles and most of the sea reptiles disappeared, too.

WHERE CAN *YOU* SEE RIVERS OF ROCK?

Did you know . . .

Scientists who study volcanoes are called volcanologists. They get their name from Vulcan, the Roman god of fire.

Volcanoes are weak spots in Earth's surface, or crust. Sometimes, a red-hot river of lava pours out of a volcano and flows down its sides. The runny rock can reach temperatures of more than 1,800°F (1,000°C)—much, much hotter than an oven—and it can flow faster than you can run!

Did you know · · ·

Tiger sharks are killing machines even before they are born. Inside their mother's body, the two strongest babies eat up all their brothers and sisters.

Some sharks give birth to live young. Others lay eggs and leave their babies to hatch on their own. Out in the ocean, baby sharks are at risk from larger predators—including other sharks. Lemon sharks are born in shallow lagoons. They live there in safety for about seven years, hanging around with other young of the same size.

WHERE DO ANGELS, CLOWNS, AND PARROTS LIVE?

Did you know . . .

Some parrotfish coat themselves in mucus at night. These sticky "pajamas" seem to make the fish harder for predators to sniff out.

Angelfish, clown fish (anemone fish), and parrotfish are just some of the thousands of beautiful animals that live on coral reefs. Reefs grow in shallow water in tropical parts of the world. They contain millions of tiny animals called coral polyps. As each polyp dies, it leaves behind its hard, stony skeleton, building up the reef.

WHERE DO I GET MY BALANCE FROM?

Your ears are not just listening machines—they also help you stay balanced. When you tilt or rotate your head, balance organs in your inner ears send a message to your brain. Then your brain can tell your body how to move so that you do not wobble around.

Did you know . . .

The smallest bone in your body is in the ear. It is called the stapes, and it is only 2 millimeters long—small enough to sit on top of this letter "e."

WHERE DO ELEPHANTS GLOW IN THE DARK?

For the Sri Lankan festival of Esala Perahera, people dress elephants in beautiful costumes and decorate them with strings of electric lights. There is a nighttime procession of more than 50 elephants, along with thousands of drummers and dancers.

Did you know . . .

The Esala Perahera is a Buddhist festival. The elephants carry a holy relic—believed to be the tooth of Buddha himself—through the streets.

WHERE DO BEARS GO IN THE WINTER?

Black and brown bears live in the cold forests of the far north. They escape the winter chill by snuggling up in their dens, which might be in a cave or a hollow tree. They sleep most of the time, living off the body fat they stored up during the summer.

WHERE IS THE WORLD OF THE ICE GIANTS?

Did you know . . .
The World of the Ice Giants was discovered in 1879 and opened to the public in 1912. In places, the ice is 65 feet (20 meters) thick.

You will have to take a trip to Austria to visit the World of the Ice Giants, or Eisriesenwelt, the world's biggest system of ice caves. Ice caves form inside solid rock as caves' rock walls become coated in ice that stays frozen all year long.

WHERE IS IT NIGHT ALL DAY LONG?

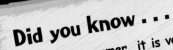
During the winter months, the lands around the poles do not see the Sun at all. The Sun is so low in the sky that it is hidden below the horizon. This makes the days cold and dark—even at noon. In Scandinavia in northern Europe, children go to and from school by the light of the Moon or stars.

WHERE IS THE TWILIGHT ZONE?

A cave is a mini world of different light and temperature zones. Some sunlight and rainfall reaches the entrance zone, and the temperature there is similar to that outside. The twilight zone is darker, damper, and cooler. Bats like to shelter there. The dark zone of the inner cave is even cooler and wetter, and it is always pitch-black.

Did you know . . .

The record for the biggest bat colony belongs to Bracken Cave, Texas. More than 20 million Mexican free-tailed bats spend part of the year there.

WHERE MIGHT *YOU* FIND A PHARAOH?

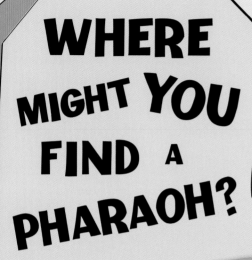

Did you know . . .

Many pharaohs were buried in desert tombs in a place called the Valley of the Kings. The most famous tomb was for the boy king Tutankhamen.

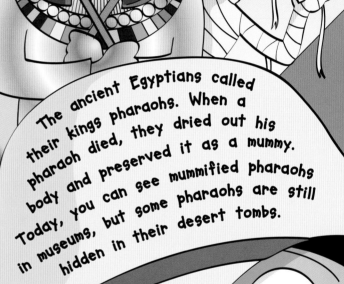

The ancient Egyptians called their kings pharaohs. When a pharaoh died, they dried out his body and preserved it as a mummy. Today, you can see mummified pharaohs in museums, but some pharaohs are still hidden in their desert tombs.

WHERE ARE THE PYRAMIDS?

The pyramids were huge tombs for dead pharaohs. There are pyramids at more than 80 sites in Egypt, but the most famous three are at Giza on the banks of the Nile River. They were built more than 4,500 years ago for the pharaohs Khufu (Cheops), Khafra, and Menkaure.

Did you know . . .

A huge statue of a sphinx guards the pyramids of Giza. It has a lion's body and a human head. The statue is huge—more than 230 feet (70 meters) long and 65 feet (20 meters) high.

WHERE DO RAINBOWS HAPPEN?

Did you know . . .

The colors in a rainbow always appear in the same order: red, orange, yellow, green, blue, indigo, and violet.

You can see a rainbow when there are water droplets in the air, such as in mist or rain, and when the Sun is behind you and at a low angle. Sunlight is actually made up of many colors. When it shines through water droplets, the light splits into all of these colors.

18

WHERE DOES IT RAIN FOR A MONTH?

Did you know . . .

Mawsynram in India is the wettest place on Earth. An average of 467 inches (11,870 millimeters) of rain falls there every year, most of it in the monsoon season.

Many tropical countries have a dry season and a wet season. Some parts of India and Southeast Asia have long, heavy downpours called mongoons. Big, black clouds blow in from the ocean during the summer months. Once the rain starts, it can last for weeks, flooding the fields and streets.

WHERE DOES CHOCOLATE GROW ON TREES?

Chocolate is made from the seeds of the cacao tree. Sadly, this tree does not grow everywhere—only in hot, wet places. The cacao tree originated in Central and South America. Today, it also grows on plantations in Southeast Asia and West Africa.

WHERE DO PLANTS GROW?

Did you know . . .

Plants come in many shapes and sizes. They range from tiny waterweeds, no bigger than a period, to towering trees.

There are about 380,000 different kinds of plants on Earth, and they grow just about everywhere—in fields and forests, deserts and mountains, rivers and lakes. Besides air, the two things plants need are sunlight and water, so they cannot grow in places that are completely dark or dry.

WHERE DOES MY FOOD GO?

Did you know . . .

Your small intestine, where the nutrients in your food pass into your body, is an amazing 20 feet (6 meters) long!

When you swallow food, it passes down your throat and into your stomach, where it is mashed into a kind of soup. This "soup" is squeezed along a winding tube called your small intestine. By now, the useful pieces of food are tiny enough to be taken into your blood and carried around your body, giving it energy to live and grow.

WHERE DO INVENTORS GET THEIR IDEAS?

Inventors get ideas for their inventions in many different places. Some of them study plants and animals to see how they have solved their problems. Others look at ideas from other places or from the past. Very few ideas come from out of the blue.

Did you know . . .

Safety pins were introduced about 160 years ago, but they have a much longer history. The inventor copied the idea from the ancient Egyptians.

23

WHERE DOES COAL COME FROM?

Did you know . . .
The period from 355 to 290 million years ago is known as the Coal Age. Some amazing plants grew during this time, including gigantic club mosses that towered 130 feet (40 meters) high.

Most of the coal that we burn today was formed from the fossilized remains of prehistoric forests that covered the land between 355 and 290 million years ago. Layers of plant matter built up on the beds of shallow seas. Over millions of years, the plant matter was pressed down and transformed into layers of hard, black rock.

WHERE CAN I SAVE ENERGY?

Did you know . . .

Old-style incandescent light bulbs usually work for about 1,000 hours at the most. Energy-saving bulbs have a life span of up to 15,000 hours!

We use energy all the time—it powers our cars and lights and heats our homes. One way to save energy is to walk or ride your bike to school instead of going by car. Other ways include turning off the lights when you leave a room and keeping heat from escaping using insulation or a "draft excluder" (below). You can also replace any old-style light bulbs in your home with energy-saving bulbs (below, left) instead.

WHERE DOES UNDERWATER GRASS GROW?

Did you know . . .

Despite their plantlike appearance, seaweeds are not plants. They belong to a different group of living things called algae.

Sea grass grows in shallow water and is the only ocean plant that has flowers. Its leaves are long and green, like blades of grass. Sea grass often forms underwater "meadows," where dugongs come to graze. Dugongs are also known as sea cows.

WHERE IS THE BIGGEST ANIMAL?

Did you know . . .

The largest land animal is the African elephant. An adult male weighs almost 8 tons—the same as five compact cars.

The blue whale is the biggest animal ever to have lived on Earth, and it lives in the world's oceans. It is so long that eight elephants could stand along its back and so heavy that it weighs as much as 100 cars! On land, an animal as big as the blue whale would collapse under its own weight. In the ocean, the water supports its body better.

WHERE DOES THE BIGGEST REPTILE LIVE?

Did you know . . .

In short bursts, a saltwater crocodile can zip through the water at speeds of up to 26 feet (8 meters) per second.

The biggest living reptile is the saltwater crocodile of tropical Asia and Australia. As its name suggests, it is at home in salt water and may swim far out to sea. During the wet season, however, it spends its time inland in freshwater rivers and swamps. The "saltie" lurks near the water's edge, waiting for unsuspecting prey to come near.

WHERE IS THE LONGEST RIVER?

Did you know . . .

Hippos used to be common all along the Nile. They are the second-largest land animals after elephants. Hippo males are as long as a car!

The world's longest river is the Nile, which flows up through North Africa. It is about 4,100 miles (6,650 kilometers) long—155 miles (250 kilometers) longer than the Amazon River in South America.

WHERE DO ANGELS FALL?

Did you know . . .

The Venezuelan name for the falls is Kerepakupai Merú, which means "waterfall of the deepest place" in a local language.

Angel Falls in Venezuela, South America, is the world's tallest waterfall, measuring 3,212 feet (979 meters). The wind blows much of the water into mist. The falls are named after an American adventurer, James Angel, who crashed his plane nearby in the 1930s.

WHERE DOES THE SUN GO AT NIGHT?

Over the course of a day, the Sun seems to travel across the sky, from east to west, and then sink below the horizon. The Sun has set, and it is night! This happens because Earth is turning all the time. While your half of the planet is turned away from the Sun, experiencing night, the opposite half of the world is facing the Sun, experiencing daytime.

Did you know . . .

The ancient Greeks believed that the Sun was a god, riding across the sky in his blazing chariot.

WHERE DO KOALAS LIVE?

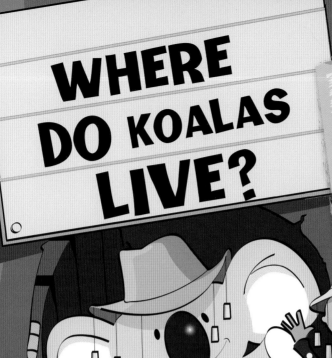

Did you know . . .

Koalas get water from their food and rarely need to drink. Their name comes from an Australian Aboriginal word meaning "no drink."

Koalas are picky creatures. They eat only the leaves and young shoots of eucalyptus trees. So the only place koalas live, in the wild, is in the eucalyptus forests of Australia.

WHERE IS THERE LAND BUT NO COUNTRIES?

Did you know . . .

No one lives in Antarctica except for a few hundred scientists. They study rocks, the weather, and plant and animal life.

The vast, frozen land around the South Pole is called Antarctica. It is not a country because it has no people, no government, and no flag. Many countries have signed an agreement promising to keep Antarctica as a wilderness where scientists from all nations can study.

WHERE WAS THE HEAVIEST SNOWFALL?

38

Did you know . . .

The largest single snowstorm on record was in Alaska in 1955. It lasted for five days and dumped almost 175 inches (4,450 millimeters) of snow.

In the 12-month period from February 19, 1971, to February 18, 1972, an amazing 1,122 inches (28,499 millimeters) of snow fell on Mount Rainier in Washington. That is about the same depth of snow as 19 people standing on one another's heads!

WHERE DID BIRDS COME FROM?

Did you know . . .

Most early birds are known from only one fossil. However, more than 1,000 fossils of the dino bird *Confuciusornis* have been found.

Dinosaurs may not have been able to fly, but scientists agree that birds evolved from small, feathered dinosaurs called maniraptorans. The oldest known dino bird was *Archaeopteryx*, which lived 150 million years ago in the Jurassic period. It had large hand claws and a toothed jaw.

WHERE ARE DINOSAUR FOSSILS FOUND?

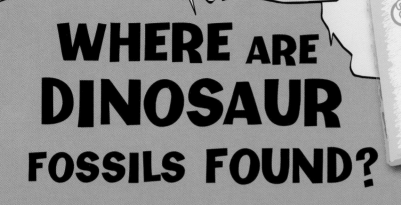

Dinosaurs lived all over Earth. Their fossils have been found in places as far apart as the U.S. and China, England and Australia—even in Antarctica. Fossils are usually buried inside rocks, so they have to be dug out.

WHERE ARE THE HIGHEST MOUNTAINS?

Did you know . . .

The longest mountain range on land is the Andes in South America. It is about 4,500 miles (7,200 kilometers) long—almost three times longer than the Himalayas.

The world's highest mountains are the Himalayas of central Asia. The mountain range has more than 110 snow-covered peaks, including Mount Everest—the world's tallest mountain—which rises to about 29,000 feet (8,850 meters). Only the toughest plants and hardiest animals can survive the extreme conditions up there.

38

WHERE DOES THE WIND GET THE WINDIEST?

Did you know . . .

Commonwealth Bay, Antarctica, is one of the windiest spots on Earth. It regularly has winds that blow faster than 150 miles (240 kilometers) per hour.

The higher you go up a mountain, the windier it gets. Winds can howl at more than 190 miles (300 kilometers) per hour at the top of the Himalayas, in Asia. It gets very chilly up there, too. For every 1,000 feet (300 meters) you climb up a mountain, the temperature drops by about 4°F (2°C).

WHERE DOES IT NEVER RAIN?

Did you know . . .

The Atacama Desert in Chile, South America, is the world's driest desert. It had no rain for 400 years. Then, in 1971, it suddenly poured!

Deserts are the world's driest places because they never—or hardly ever—have rain. Some deserts are hot and sandy. Others are cold regions with frozen soil.

WHERE ON EARTH SIZZLES THE MOST?

Did you know . . .

Around lightning, the air is briefly heated to around 54,000°F (30,000°C)—five times hotter than the surface of the Sun. Phew!

The hottest recorded temperature on Earth was in Al'Aziziyah in the Libyan Desert. On September 13, 1922, it reached 136°F (57.8°C). The remote mining town of Dallol, Ethiopia, holds the record for the hottest average temperature—93.9°F (34.4°C). No wonder no one lives there anymore!

WHERE WOULD YOU FIND A RUNNING PLANT?

The birdcage plant lives in the deserts of the American West. It puts down shallow roots in the shade of a dune to suck up what little water there is. If the sand shifts, the plant may find itself in scorching sunlight. So it leaves behind its shriveled roots and speeds off across the sand to find a new place to live. It has no legs, but its cagelike, round body allows it to roll along like a ball.

Did you know . . .

In many desert plants, the aboveground parts break away and move off to scatter seeds. They are known as tumbleweeds.

WHERE WERE THE FIRST OLYMPICS?

The first Olympic Games were held in ancient Greece as part of a festival to honor Zeus, the king of the gods. Every four years, thousands of spectators flocked to Olympia to see athletes run, box, wrestle, and race chariots (speedy, horse-drawn carts).

WHERE IS THE EYE OF A HURRICANE?

Did you know . . .

In the Far East, hurricanes are called typhoons. In India and Australia, they are known as cyclones.

With winds roaring at more than 73 miles (117 kilometers) per hour, hurricanes are the fiercest storms on Earth. At their center, however, is the eye—an area where the wind is fairly calm and there are no big storm clouds. The fast and furious hurricane winds move in a spiral around the eye.

WHERE DO EARTHQUAKES HAPPEN?

Did you know . . .

In Japanese legends, a giant catfish named Namazu triggers earthquakes by wiggling around.

Earthquakes make the ground shake. The most violent ones can move mountains, make rivers change course, and bring cities tumbling to the ground. Like volcanoes, earthquakes happen at weak spots on Earth's surface where two plates—massive sections of land—bump or grind together.

WHERE WOULD YOU FIND A FLYING WEAVER?

Did you know . . .

One kind of weaverbird, the sociable weaver, does not build its own individual nest. It teams up with other birds—as many as 100 pairs—to build one huge nest to share.

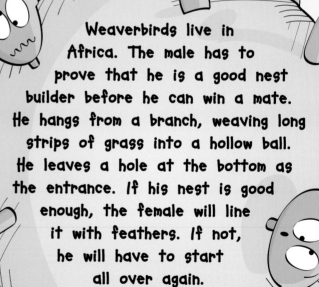

Weaverbirds live in Africa. The male has to prove that he is a good nest builder before he can win a mate. He hangs from a branch, weaving long strips of grass into a hollow ball. He leaves a hole at the bottom as the entrance. If his nest is good enough, the female will line it with feathers. If not, he will have to start all over again.

WHERE DO BIRDS LIVE IN CITIES?

Did you know . . .

Mockingbirds on the Galápagos Islands snatch hair from people's heads to line their nests. A cheap—but painful—haircut!

For many sea birds, a cliff is the perfect place to nest—safe from hunters and handy for fishing. Thousands of birds lay their eggs on the narrow ledges or nest in cracks in the rocks. With all those birds fighting for space, a cliff is like a city—crowded, smelly, and very noisy!

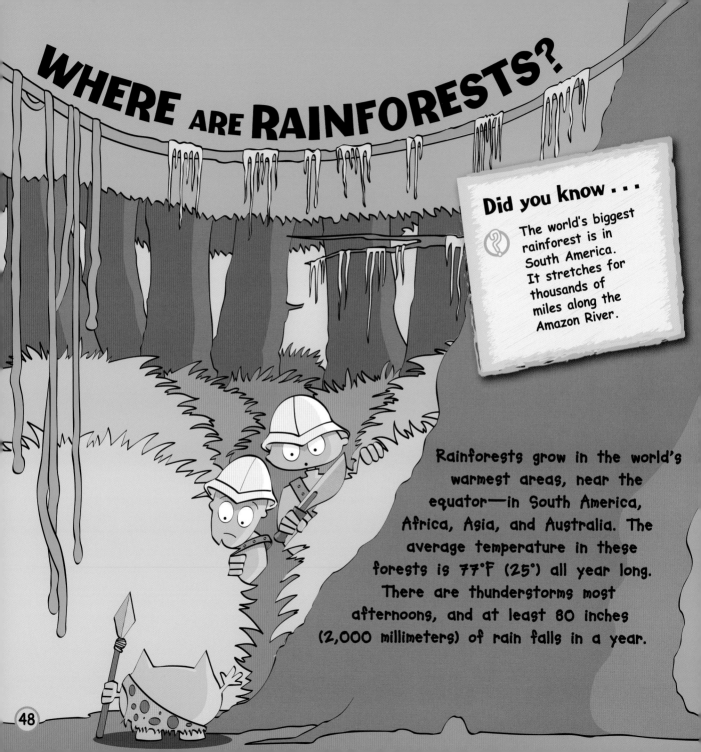

WHERE ARE RAINFORESTS?

Did you know . . .

The world's biggest rainforest is in South America. It stretches for thousands of miles along the Amazon River.

Rainforests grow in the world's warmest areas, near the equator—in South America, Africa, Asia, and Australia. The average temperature in these forests is 77°F (25°) all year long. There are thunderstorms most afternoons, and at least 80 inches (2,000 millimeters) of rain falls in a year.

WHERE IS THE BIGGEST FOREST?

Did you know . . .

This book started life as a tree trunk. Most paper comes from coniferous trees, such as spruce and pine.

The world's biggest forest is called the boreal forest. Boreal means "northern," and this forest stretches all the way across northern Europe and Asia. All of its trees are conifers—they have hard, narrow leaves called needles to withstand the cold. The boreal forest is home to brown bears, wolves, and reindeer.

WHERE IS THE LONGEST CAVE SYSTEM?

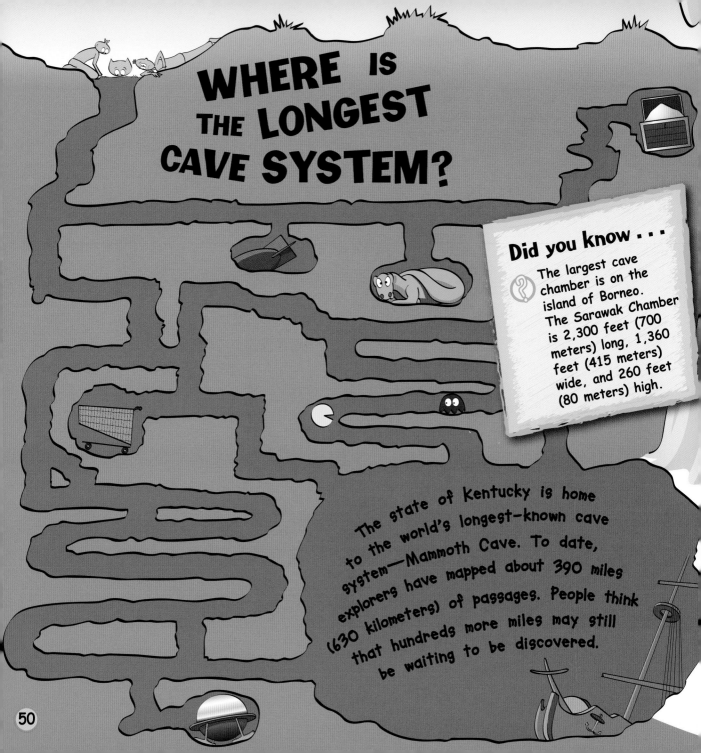

Did you know . . .

The largest cave chamber is on the island of Borneo. The Sarawak Chamber is 2,300 feet (700 meters) long, 1,360 feet (415 meters) wide, and 260 feet (80 meters) high.

The state of Kentucky is home to the world's longest-known cave system—Mammoth Cave. To date, explorers have mapped about 390 miles (630 kilometers) of passages. People think that hundreds more miles may still be waiting to be discovered.

WHERE CAN YOU PLAY SPORTS IN A CAVE?

Norway's Gjøvik Rock Cavern was blasted from the rock to house a huge underground sports stadium where hockey games were held during the 1994 Winter Olympics. At 299 feet (91 meters) long and 200 feet (61 meters) wide, it is one of the world's largest artificial rock chambers.

Did you know . . .

Not all farmers grow their crops in fields. Some use caves instead! The cool, dark conditions of a cave are perfect for growing mushrooms.

WHERE DO MEN WEAR SKIRTS?

Did you know . . .

In Scotland, each clan (family group) has its own kinds of tartan, each with a particular pattern and set of colors.

On special occasions, it is traditional for Scottish men to wear kilts. Kilts are pleated skirts made from a checked woolen cloth called tartan. They are warm, but they only come down to the knee, so they are worn with a pair of long, woolly socks.

WHERE DID CHINA COME FROM?

Although pottery was made all over the world from early times, the very finest kind, porcelain, was invented in southern China in around A.D. 600. This is why we often refer to it as "china!"

WHERE DOES IT TAKE HOURS TO DRINK TEA?

Did you know . . .

The biggest-ever tea party was held in Australia in 2005 at various places across the country. More than 280,000 people took part.

In Japan, there is a special, ancient tea ceremony called chanoyu. The tea is made so slowly, and sipped so carefully, that it really does take hours. It is not a good idea to show up to the ceremony feeling thirsty!

QUICK-QUIZ QUESTIONS

1. When did the dinosaurs disappear?

2. Volcanologists study aliens. True or false?

3. Unscramble SIP FOR HART to find a coral-reef fish.

4. Where is the smallest bone in the human body?

5. The Hindu festival of Esala Perahera features lit-up rhinos. True or false?

6. What is another name for Eisriesenwelt?

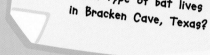

7. Which type of bat lives in Bracken Cave, Texas?

8. Unscramble MANE TUT HANK to find the name of a famous young pharaoh.

9. In what order do the seven colors of the rainbow appear?

10. How much rain falls each year in the world's wettest place?

11. How many different kinds of plants are there?

12. Unscramble CENT IN DANCES to find a type of light bulb.

13. Seaweed is a plant. True or false?

14. How long is the Great Barrier Reef?

15. Which is the world's second-longest river?

16. What do koalas eat?

17. Unscramble OY RAT CAPER HEX to find the name of one of the first birds.

18. How tall is the highest mountain on Earth?

19. Which desert had no rain for 400 years?

20. Who were the king and queen of the Greek gods?

21. What is the name of the earthquake-causing catfish in Japanese mythology?

22. Which continent is home to the largest rainforest?

23. Python Cave is the world's longest cave system. True or false?

24. Which country hosted the 1994 Winter Olympics?

25. What would you be served at a chanoyu?

QUICK-QUIZ ANSWERS

1. About 65 million years ago.

2. False. They study volcanoes.

3. SIP FOR HART = Parrotfish.

4. Inside the ear.

5. False. Esala Perahera is a Buddhist festival, and the animals on parade are elephants.

6. The World of the Ice Giants.

7. The Mexican free-tailed bat.

8. MANE TUT HANK = Tutankhamen.

9. Red, orange, yellow, green, blue, indigo, violet.

10. An average of 467 inches (11,870 millimeters).

11. About 380,000.

12. CENT IN DANCES = Incandescent.

13. False. Seaweed is an alga, not a plant.

14. More than 1,240 miles (2,000 kilometers) long.

15. The Amazon River.

16. Eucalyptus leaves and shoots.

17. OY RAT CAPER HEX = Archaeopteryx.

18. About 29,000 feet (8,850 meters) tall.

19. The Atacama Desert in Chile.

20. Zeus and Hera.

21. Namazu.

22. South America (the Amazon rainforest).

23. False. Mammoth Cave is the longest cave system.

24. Norway.

25. Tea.

TRICKY WORDS

ALGAE
Algae is the overall name for a group of very simple living things. Seaweeds are algae.

ANCIENT EGYPTIANS
A people who lived in Egypt, from around 5,000 to 2,000 years ago.

ANCIENT GREEKS
A people who lived in and around Greece, from around 3,000 to 1,600 years ago.

ANCIENT ROMANS
A people from Italy who lived around 2,000 years ago in Europe, Africa, and Asia.

ANTARCTICA
Earth's icy, southernmost area around the South Pole.

CONTINENT
One of Earth's seven main landmasses—North America, South America, Europe, Africa, Asia, Australia, and Antarctica.

CRUST
The outer layer of planet Earth, on which we live.

DESERT
A dry region with little plant life.

DINO BIRD
An animal that shares characteristics with dinosaurs and modern birds. Birds evolved from dinosaurs hundreds of millions of years ago.

DUGONG
A plant-eating sea mammal found in shallow, warm waters of the Indian and Pacific oceans.

EQUATOR
The imaginary line that circles the middle of Earth.

EVOLVE
To change from one species to another over millions of years by passing on useful characteristics from one generation to the next.

FOSSIL
The remains of a plant or creature that existed long ago. Fossils are usually formed from the hard parts of an animal or plant, such as teeth, bones, or shells. They are created when, for example, animal bones sink into mud, which then hardens gradually into rock.

HORIZON
The line, in the distance, at which Earth's surface and the sky appear to meet.

HURRICANE
A strong storm that forms over warm oceans. Its winds can travel at more than 73 miles (117 kilometers) per hour.

INCANDESCENT LIGHT BULB
A light bulb that makes light by heating a thin, metal wire—called a filament—so that it glows. The filament is protected inside a glass bulb.

INVENTOR
A person who is the first to think of or create something, such as a machine.

LAGOON
A pool of salt water separated from the ocean—for example, by a reef.

LAVA
Liquid rock that spurts from volcanoes or cracks in Earth's crust (surface layer).

LEGEND
A story that has been told for a long time.

MAYA
An ancient people who lived in Mexico and northern Central America, from around 3,500 to 1,000 years ago.

MONSOON
Occurs during the wet season in India and Southeast Asia. A seasonal wind, also called the monsoon, brings rain.

MUCUS
A slimy substance squeezed out by an animal's glands.

OLYMPIC GAMES
International sporting events that take place every four years. The first Olympics were held in ancient Greece.

PLANTATION
A large farm where only one crop—for example, cacao, coffee, or tea—is grown for money.

PREDATOR
An animal that hunts and eats other animals.

PREHISTORIC
Describes the period of history before our written records began.

PREY
An animal that is hunted and eaten by other animals.

PYRAMID
A large, stone building with four triangular sides. The ancient Egyptians built pyramids as tombs.

REEF
A long line of rock, sand, or coral that lies just beneath the surface of the ocean.

REPTILE
An animal with a backbone and scaly skin. Most reptiles lay eggs on land, but some give birth to live young.

SHALE
Fine rock formed from hardened mud and clay.

SPHINX
An ancient Egyptian statue with a lion's body and a human or animal head.

TARTAN
A woven cloth from Scotland, made from wool and patterned with checks and stripes of different thicknesses and colors.

VOLCANO
A vent (hole) in the surface or crust of a planet through which gas, ash, and molten rock escape. The material that erupts can build up to form a mountain.

VOLCANOLOGIST
Someone whose job it is to study volcanoes.

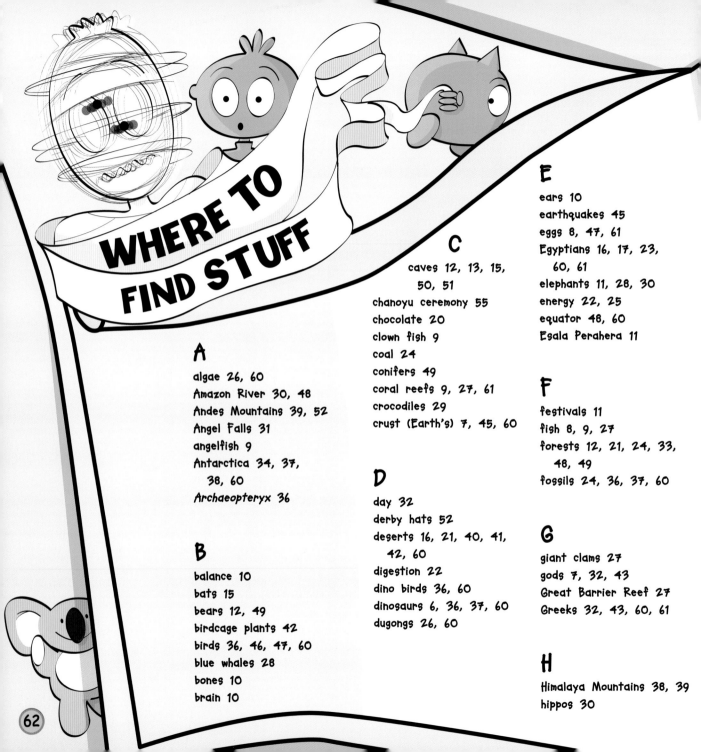

WHERE TO FIND STUFF

A

algae 26, 60
Amazon River 30, 48
Andes Mountains 39, 52
Angel Falls 31
angelfish 9
Antarctica 34, 37, 38, 60
Archaeopteryx 36

B

balance 10
bats 15
bears 12, 49
birdcage plants 42
birds 36, 46, 47, 60
blue whales 28
bones 10
brain 10

C

caves 12, 13, 15, 50, 51
chanoyu ceremony 55
chocolate 20
clown fish 9
coal 24
conifers 49
coral reefs 9, 27, 61
crocodiles 29
crust (Earth's) 7, 45, 60

D

day 32
derby hats 52
deserts 16, 21, 40, 41, 42, 60
digestion 22
dino birds 36, 60
dinosaurs 6, 36, 37, 60
dugongs 26, 60

E

ears 10
earthquakes 45
eggs 8, 47, 61
Egyptians 16, 17, 23, 60, 61
elephants 11, 28, 30
energy 22, 25
equator 48, 60
Esala Perahera 11

F

festivals 11
fish 8, 9, 27
forests 12, 21, 24, 33, 48, 49
fossils 24, 36, 37, 60

G

giant clams 27
gods 7, 32, 43
Great Barrier Reef 27
Greeks 32, 43, 60, 61

H

Himalaya Mountains 38, 39
hippos 30

hockey 30
hurricanes 44, 60

I

ice caves 13
intestines 22
inventors 23, 60

JK

kilts 53
koalas 33

L

lagoons 8, 60
lava 7, 61
light bulbs 25, 60
lightning 41

M

Mammoth Cave 50
Maya 20, 61
mockingbirds 47
monsoons 19, 61
moray eels 27
mountains 21, 38,
   39, 45

mucus 9, 61
mummies 16
mushrooms 51

N

nests 46, 47
night 32
Nile River 17, 30

O

oceans and seas 8, 9,
   19, 26, 27, 28, 29,
   47, 60, 61
Olympic Games 43, 51, 61

PQ

parrotfish 9
pharaohs 16, 17
plantations 20, 61
plants 6, 20, 21, 23,
   24, 26, 33, 34, 39,
   42, 49, 60
poles 14, 34, 37, 38, 60
porcelain 54
predators 8, 61
pyramids 17, 61

R

rain 15, 18, 19, 40,
   48, 61
rainbows 18
rainforests 48
reptiles 6, 29, 61
rivers 17, 21, 29, 30, 45
Romans 7, 61

S

Sarawak Chamber 51
sea birds 47
sea grasses 26
seasons 12, 14, 19, 29, 61
seaweeds 26, 60
sharks 8
snow 35
sphinxes 17, 61
sports 43, 51, 61
storms 19, 35, 38, 41,
   44, 48, 60
summer 12, 14, 19
Sun 6, 14, 18, 32, 41

T

tartans 53, 61
tea 55
tumbleweeds 42

UV

volcanoes 7, 61
volcanologists 7, 61

WXYZ

waterfalls 31
weaverbirds 46
winds 19, 38, 44, 61
winter 12, 14
wool 52, 53
World of the Ice Giants 13